WE ARE

ONE

THE POWER OF THE
CONSCIOUS MIND
AND OUR INTERCONNECTION
TO ALL THINGS

EDGAR MITCHELL
APOLLO 14
LUNAR MODULE PILOT

BOOKS FROM CAROL MERSCH
AND PEN-L PUBLISHING

Reflections of the Moon

Apostles of Apollo

Undaunted

We Are One

WE ARE ONE

EDGAR MITCHELL
APOLLO 14
LUNAR MODULE PILOT

**THE SIXTH MAN
TO WALK ON THE MOON**

**FOUNDER OF
THE INSTITUTE OF NOETIC SCIENCES
CO-FOUNDER OF THE
ASSOCIATION OF SPACE EXPLORERS**

COMPILED BY CAROL MERSCH

The following pages contain a commentary by Apollo 14
Lunar Module Pilot Dr. Edgar Mitchell in 2006, as
recorded by Sheila Mitchell, and combined here with
other commentaries with his permission.

Printed and bound in the U.S.A.

ISBN: 978-1-68313-221-9
Library of Congress Control Number: 2020939531

Pen-L Publishing
Fayetteville, Arkansas
www.Pen-L.com

Books may be ordered from booksellers or by contacting:
the publisher at Info@Pen-L.com

CONTENTS

AUTHOR'S NOTE

In 1978 I sat riveted in my chair in a conference hall in Orlando, Florida. The keynote speaker had just said something that was almost inconceivable. The speaker, Navy Lt. Commander Edgar Dean Mitchell, a handsome, soft-spoken forty-something, had just recently returned from the Apollo 14 lunar landing where he became the sixth man to walk on the Moon. I had been sent to the conference by my company as a "bon-bon" for doing a good job on a software project. The software had been purchased by a major software vendor, Insight International Computing. Mitchell was a partner in the firm.

He spoke in almost a stoic monotone about his venture to the Moon—and then about his experience on the ground during recovery of the ill-fated Apollo 13. He described the intense, hurried activity in Mission Control as he and T.K. (Ken) Mattingly slid into the lunar and command module simulators, methodically rehearsing every imaginable scenario for a manual reentry of the craft—every switch, every item on board that might be used, duct tape, cardboard—to save the lives of their comrades.

When they climbed into the simulators, the odds were ten to one against the Apollo 13 crew surviving the ordeal. Ingenuity and intuition kicked in as the two, surrounded by an adept NASA team, tested modified control procedures and rudimentary manual schemes for conserving the depleted

Apollo 13 resources of power, water, and oxygen, and for the tricky manual re-entry of the piggy-backed space craft.

No one had ever envisioned or trained for the complex sequence of failures that would occur—at least not all of them at once. Even in their wildest conjecture they had never conceived that the command module would re-enter earth orbit wagging the cumbersome lunar module behind it, with no computerized controls and less power than a 12-volt battery.

Twenty-two hours after the accident, Apollo 13, wounded and battered, emerged from around the moon headed for the long journey home. The spacecraft was gyrating wildly as the crew attempted to target the narrow re-entry trajectory in the crosshairs using only the cusp of the sun aligned with earth as a reference.

Meanwhile, a world that had previously grown weary of the U.S. space program began tuning in their radios and televisions to witness the crisis. Word that Apollo 13 was in danger had spread throughout the world from Tokyo to Detroit to Tel Aviv. Headlines from Toronto to Tokyo blared the message that Apollo was in danger. News bulletins cut into radio and TV programs to report new developments. Crowds gathered anywhere there was a television set. In Rome, Pope Paul VI prayed for the astronaut's return before an audience of ten thousand people. At a religious festival in India, pilgrims numbering ten times as many offered prayers for the astronauts. It is estimated that one-third of the world's population was focused on the event.

And the odds of recovery began to rise.

As the world watched in hope, three orange and white parachutes blossomed over the Pacific Ocean, and the Apollo 13 crew splashed down within eyesight of the rescue ship, one of the closest splashdowns of any spacecraft.

What brought Apollo 13 back? It can arguably be said that it was the expertise of man-made invention and brilliant minds that brought NASA to "their finest hour." But Mitchell, a PhD physicist steeped in hard science, closed his remarks by saying, when all was said and done, *"It was the power of thousands of praying minds that pulled the Apollo 13 spacecraft back to earth."*

He then thanked the audience and left the podium.

I was dumbstruck. This soft-spoken man with a reported I.Q. of 180 had just taken a 180-degree turn into the esoteric world of quantum entanglement. I sat glued to my chair. People around me were rising from their seats and shuffling out the door. Was I the only one who heard that?

For nearly twenty-five years those words would run through my mind, wondering what he meant by them and why he said them. Where was he now and what was he doing? Was he dead? Did he know what a profound impression his words had made on someone? Would he care? Only one way to find out. I had to track him down. I had to look into his eyes and have him tell me.

In April 2002 that happened.

You will find in these pages an introduction to the man I met that morning at a quiet breakfast on a beach in Palm Beach, Florida.

And my life was forever changed.

PROLOGUE

As a result of my experience in space, any doubts that I had about the Universe being a Divine Creation evaporated, to be replaced with the certainty that the physical Universe and its creatures are the result of divine thought and purpose. I view the spiritual aspect of life as the most important part of human experience and believe that growth in the spiritual dimensions is limited only by our individual unwillingness to see beyond our fears and selfish interests. To seek tranquility and joy by realizing one's true spiritual nature is the ultimate goal of all life.

Apollo 14 Edgar Mitchell
In a note to Apollo 15 Jim Irwin
August 23, 1978

FOREWORD

More than 100 billion people have walked the face of the Earth. Twelve have walked on the moon. One of those was Edgar Mitchell.

On January 31, 1971, Navy Captain Dr. Edgar Mitchell embarked on a journey into outer space, resulting in his becoming the sixth man to walk on the moon. The Apollo 14 mission was NASA's third manned lunar landing. This historic journey ended safely nine days later on February 9, 1971. It was an audacious time in the history of mankind. For Mitchell, however, the most extraordinary journey was yet to come.

What he did not mention to NASA or the press was his transformative experience in the *Apollo 14* command module during the long journey back to earth. Up to this point, the astronauts had been busy, minute by minute. But now, in the quiet of the command module, drifting silently in lunar orbit, he found himself gazing out the window at the celestial panorama unfolding before him.

Mitchell's upbringing had ingrained him with theories about religion and the Bible that eventually became too dogmatic for his prying scientific mind. From his perspective, the Bible had been used more as a basis for war than peace, and one he could no longer accept at face value. But his journey to the moon had molded his lack of belief into something new. "This is a sight that bores deep into the soul and shakes the foundation of your being."

Mitchell had an awakening—a feeling that there was a greater being, a guiding hand, and that science and spirituality were not two different dimensions of reality. They were, in fact, one and the same. This transforming experience sent him on a search for what he now saw as a more likely truth: the presence of a cosmic conscience and order in the universe—a Divine Mind controlling every fabric of our being, from our mental molecules to the vast empires of the universe. His journey toward the intersection of science and spirituality would consume the rest of his life.

He left NASA in 1973 to found the Institute of Noetic Sciences, a worldwide organization dedicated to the research of global awareness and universal consciousness.

What follows in these pages are Mitchell's firsthand account of the experience and thoughts that enveloped him during his long return to earth from the moon. What Mitchell also did not mention to NASA was what he revealed to me in 2005—that he had carried the first Bible to the surface of the moon.

Over the years, his scientific studies of astrophysics and astronautics blended with a broader understanding of the realities of unseen forces to convince him that his being and that of all life are intertwined throughout time and space. They were one and the same.

In 2005 he wrote:

"For many years after founding my Institute of Noetic Sciences, the stress of growing an avant-garde nonprofit foundation while raising and educating children and providing for a family created some interesting and challenging years. I had to revamp my entire psychology toward money, economics, and life itself to keep my balance and sanity. I learned to 'trust the process'— otherwise stated in more conventional terms as 'let go and let God.' In 30 years, now, it hasn't failed me."

Carol Mersch, Compiler

This book is dedicated to those who dare to
believe in the power of the conscious mind
to change to world.

"We are limited even in the body only by
what we believe about ourselves."

– Edgar Mitchell

THE JOURNEY BEGINS

Although I have recorded the story of Apollo 14 and my impressions of that flight else-where, there is a particular experience that occurred on the flight that I think is worthy of a separate telling. It is a story all its own. It is the story of the powerful emotional experience I had in space as I looked upon the beauty of our planet as it appears in the cosmos. It is the story of the effect on my thinking and my life as I came face to face with the deeper meaning of man's existence from the vantage point of being one of the privileged few to leave the confines of Mother Earth and to venture out into the void of space to see our world from afar.

I would like to share that story with you.

Edgar Mitchell
Lunar Module Pilot, Apollo 14

WE ARE ONE

Imagine with me the following scene:

We're in the cabin of Apollo 14 having just left lunar orbit after a very exciting, fulfilling, and successful exploration of the lunar surface. The rugged moonscape is receding in the background, the features slowly becoming smaller as we watch out the cabin window. We are several thousand miles away now and the little planet is clearly the sphere in our field of view. We are tired but exhilarated, not having eaten in twelve hours or slept in twenty-two. Our missions in lunar orbit and on the lunar surface were highly successful. We have completed all the assigned tasks and we're now on our way home—gratified, happy, relaxed, and very tired.

The crew tasks are light, giving us a chance to rest, to make up the sleep deficit of the last few days, recover from sore muscles, and bask in the satisfaction of a mission well done. The spacecraft is small, but with ample room for the three of us to float around to our workstations in the weightlessness of space. A small amount of dust and debris float in the cabin, left over from the transfer of dusty pressure suits and equipment brought into the lunar module from the moon's surface. It will be several hours before all those tiny loose particles will be trapped by the filters in the air conditioning system. I take this opportunity to look out a spacecraft window to catch a glimpse of planet Earth—our home planet—as it moves past each of five windows in turn, for we are rotating slowly like beef on a barbeque spit, to allow the Sun's powerful rays to be equally distributed over the spacecraft. In fact, we call it the "barbeque mode," even though the official name is "passive thermal control," PCT for short. The official names are cold and technical, and usually tongue twisters, so we frequently use more familiar terms.

I take the opportunity of the relaxed workload on the journey home to contemplate Earth. To view the little planet that is our spaceship, we the people of Earth. It is a rare event.

I feel privileged to be one of the first of only a few persons in all history to leave the planet and be able to view it from afar—from deep space. To get out of the trees and view the forest. But of equal importance, to have a few private moments to take in the scene and to muse upon its deeper existence. It's a beautiful little planet, blue and white, and set in the black emptiness of the universe, surrounded by billions of bright stars. Stars in such profusion, but which we never see from the surface of the Earth without a telescope because our atmosphere screens out their light.

This is a sight that bores deep into the soul and shakes the foundation of your being.

Perhaps you have seen some of the photographs that some of my colleagues have been able to take of planet Earth from deep space. Perhaps with those photographs, and with your imagination, you can capture the profundity and the magnificence that we saw from that vantage point. All of my adult life had been as an engineer, a scientist, a test pilot, a naval officer, working daily with mathematics, exotic equipment, the hard facts of the technical professions—and the realities of war.

It is accepted knowledge that we reside on a small planet, circling an average sun, way out on the spiral arm of a rather mundane galaxy, which is only one of a million we can see in our telescope. Distances are measured in light years—not in miles—or even millions of miles. Those are the facts of our modern knowledge, most of which has been discovered in the last one hundred years of man's existence, facts that every school child of the space age learned in elementary school. But facts that my generation didn't really think about until adulthood, when they were thrust upon our professional lives.

However, like many of you, throughout my life I have pondered the burning questions that have intrigued and troubled mankind for thousands of years—that have fueled the fires of our inquisitive searching—leaving us in the twentieth century to overcome the gravitational pull and carry out this venture to our nearest neighbor, the moon. Questions like:

Why am I here? What is our purpose?

Are we simply a step above the animals? Are the planets and stars really formed by the random and accidental collision of matter coming together in space because of gravitation? Is it really all an accident . . . or is there much, much more?

Is, indeed, the universe created? Are *we* divinely created creatures? Or is there a master plan that humankind and the other inhabitants of planet Earth are carrying out? I contemplated these questions while looking at the magnificence of planet Earth. Earth, floating in the vastness of space, a grain of sand in the cosmic sea. And as I did so, an experience occurred which firmly and completely calmed my mind on these troublesome questions.

In an instant I knew for certain that what I was seeing was no accident. That it did not occur randomly and without a plan. That life did not, by accident, arise from the primordial earthly sea.

It was as though my awareness reached out to touch the farthest star and I was aware of being an integral part of the entire universe for one brief instant. How magnificent. How perfect. How loving. How harmonious. How orderly was this universe that we inhabit.

*As tiny as our physical bodies are on the scale
of the universe, our minds can reach out to
become one with all that is.*

Any questions that my curious mind
might have had about our progress,
about our destiny, about the nature of the
universe, suddenly melted away as I experienced that oneness. I could reach out
and touch the farthest parts and experience
the vast reaches of the universe. It was
clear that those tiny pinpoints of light, in
brilliant profusion, were a part of the
plan. They were linked together as part of
the whole as they framed and formed a
backdrop for this fragile planet Earth. I
knew that we were not alone in this
universe. That Earth was only one of
millions, perhaps billions, of planets like
our own, with intelligent life, all playing a
role in that great divine plan in the
evolution of life.

This experience was euphoric, uplifting. Mystics would call it a "mystical experience." Psychologist would call it a "peak experience." Theologians would say it was "touching the face of God."

But none of those words quite do justice to the indescribable feeling of knowing, for one instant, that certainly life had purpose.

That the universe had a plan, had direction, had harmony, was structured and organized and moved with the thought of God, and not as a lifeless, inanimate machine on which we are accidental passengers.

However, as I continued to gaze at Earth, the euphoria, the sense of oneness, of wholeness, of participation, changed into a feeling of deep despair—the darkest, blackest despair. The most agonizing emotional pain I had ever felt, as I

contemplated man and his condition on Earth, behaving like ancient warring tribes fighting over food and territorial rights—or like lemmings rushing toward the sea—or like spoiled children fighting over favorite toys—than like the evolved, enlightened beings with a destiny that I now knew we were.

How painful to know that beneath that blue atmosphere and clouds were my people, the crew of spaceship Earth, in disharmony and disarray, egocentrically, lustily, hatefully, greedily destroying themselves and each other for lack of vision—for lack of understanding of what mankind really is.

We are universal beings. We are stewards and keepers of spaceship Earth. Not the spoiled, self-serving brats we all portray. A species not knowing our own potential.

*Not sensing the omnipotence of God nor the
limitlessness of our creative capability.*

Not recognizing our God-given gifts of
intelligence, intuition, creativity—that the
spirit within us is the guiding force that
makes mankind great. It enables us to rise
above our more base instincts to become
the creative, intelligent, loving creatures
of the universe that is our true reality.
Unwilling to rise above the angry,
warring, self-serving mentality that so
often directs our behavior.

This despair was black and painful.
But fortunately for me, my duties aboard
the spacecraft interrupted these thoughts
and caused me to return to my tasks and
to function as a member of our home-
ward bound crew. However, for the next
thirty hours, in my moments of rest and
in between crew chores, the experience
was repeated. The high. The euphoria.

The knowledge of man's oneness with God and his destiny in the Universe. To be followed by the despair—the blackness of mood that the recognition that we are hurting only ourselves as we continue to ignore our potential and continue to ignore our higher nature and our spiritual selves, in favor of the self-serving behavior that mankind too often indulges in.

Buckminster Fuller's analogy of spaceship Earth appeared so apt. We of Apollo 14 were only three with responsibility conserving our resources—working as a team—following the flight plan if we were to return successfully to Earth. It is no different with spaceship Earth. Except that the crew numbers billions and the craft is a planet and the resources greater, but ample, although still limited and finite. It is clear to me that the crew of spaceship Earth can no longer afford wastefulness, disharmony, and mutiny any more than we three could.

For Earth to survive as a planet and to provide for the nurturing, the growth, and well being of the inhabitants, then we, humankind, must rise to the challenge of learning to be stewards to Earth and to each other.

Not the ravagers and pillagers of its resources, torn out wastefully for exaggerated, self-serving desires. We need to work cooperatively with Earth, not as manipulators. We no longer can follow the patterns of our earlier, more primitive, infantile years on Earth. Patterns of our generations before, who believed because we were few in number and the Earth was so large that its resources would last forever. Who believed—and we still believe—that conquest creates conformity. And threat produces peace.

The sages and peacemakers who have dotted our history and helped pioneer the knowledge and growth of civilization—where has their message gone? For this vision says nothing that is new. The message is old, but still largely unheeded.

The veneer of our civilization is so thin that it can be shattered worldwide by a single border dispute.

No, it is quite apparent in the view from space how tiny, how fragile, how limited the Earth is if required to support a civilization determined to destroy itself by misuse of its greatest gifts. In earlier times, our limited numbers and more primitive tools prevented our juvenile passions from endangering the entire world at once. But Earth and her species could absorb the violence of humankind's adolescent behavior.

But our numerous and growing population has, in the twentieth century alone, changed us from an agricultural, primarily pastoral world dependent upon the collaboration with nature for our survival, into a post-industrial compute-rized technological society. The nuclear space age progress has certainly brought affluence and a way of life that primitive man could never have dreamed of. But we must pause and ask ourselves: Are we using it wisely?

We now possess the power and knowledge to control Earth, but have we yet the wisdom and sense of destiny necessary to control the technological genie we have set free? Has the lid to Pandora's box been opened ever so little? Has the sorcerer's apprentice opened the great book of magic?

Long after our return to Earth in February of 1971, I pondered these questions and tried to understand the experience that occurred when returning from the moon. I have sought the counsel of wise and gifted men—scholars, scientists, philosophers, mystics, and theologians in an attempt, not only to understand the insights, but to also reduce them to workable solutions.

As humans, we all think our thoughts and dream our dreams of a better and peaceful place to live.

*But thoughts, dreams, and visions alone
do not change the world.*

What they do is inspire us to a new sense of ourselves—to a new awareness of what can be done. And thus set the stage for the action that is to follow. It is appropriate to examine what has happened in that time.

As a result of my view from space, I set out to define what is the potential for mankind for meaningful and productive change.

What is it that we could become if we would dare?

The cynics say that mankind's nature will never change—we are born in passion, to war, to conquer, to seek power at the expense of others. The visionary's dreams will inspire but not convince. They say to expect the human species to change its behavior is as futile as asking a leopard to change its spots.

But what are we really? Is our nature truly just flesh and bones? A step above the animals? Or are we universal beings with great potential to determine our destiny? Along with many colleagues who share this same quest, I have redis-covered from ancient scholars, and from personal experience, a number of things about ourselves and about the universe that I would like to share.

The human is not just an intelligent animal—born to struggle for survival, needing to defend its territory against all intruders—but a limitless spiritual creature, having a body with which to achieve its goals of learning and perfection. The picture of mankind painted by the scientists of medicine, biology, chemistry, and tradi-tional psychology only describes our fragile, physical machine. Not our essence. Not our basic immortal nature.

We are limited even in the body only by what we believe about ourselves.

We function like twelve-cylinder engines operating on only one cylinder because we do not know what we are. That inefficient operation is only because we do not recognize that we have other great potentials.

We are limited only because we think we are limited.

We often say, "seeing is believing"—but precisely the opposite is true. Believing is seeing. When we change our belief, we will see ourselves differently. For tens of thousands of years we have roamed the world as nomads, fighting for survival in a harsh environment, protecting ourselves and our possessions, warring with those who seem to threaten. Only rarely have we listened to the inner voice of our true destiny. Rarely have we followed the advice of the great sages and mystics who have dotted our history. More often, we ignored that inner voice and that wise counsel, hearing what we want to hear, seeing what we want to see, to satisfy the desires of the moment. We have believed that life is hard, the environment threatening, and have thus made it so. We have felt lost and fearful, believing we are an accident beyond our control.

This is why for me it was important to experience the view from space. It helped me to experience a different reality. It settled for my mind once and for all that man is not an accident of the universe, and the universe itself a random occurrence of matter come together in space. If we are here by accident then life has no meaning—no purpose—and humankind and all the species on earth are indeed the victims of circumstance. The Flintstones and Jetsons, on the sea of existence without hope, without purpose, without destiny.

But the experience of seeing beyond, going beyond, reaching out and becoming a part of a greater understanding, even if only for a brief instant, banishes the idea of an accidental origin.

That there is purpose, that there is order and harmony in the universe, changes the entire way that we think about ourselves.

You can rightly ask: Does one have to go into space to have this perspective? Do you have to get out of the Earth in order to see beyond and see a greater reality? Of course not. Our mystics, the philosophers, the great religious teachers of all time, have been telling us throughout history of this experience. In the philosophic literature it is called "metanoia," or change of thinking. In our Christian tradition, Christ called it "to be born again." In Hindu tradition it's called "samadhi." All of these words mean to change one's consciousness and to see beyond—to perceive a greater truth.

It happened, and has happened, to thousands of people in every walk of life and in every age. That change of thinking that causes us to rise above our previous beliefs and to see ourselves in a different way. To see the world in a different way. It helps us to know that we are not the victims of the world and victims of our circumstances.

But indeed, if victims at all, we are victims of our own thinking.

For generations we have believed that power, force, and fear were the only workable tools to motivate people and to shape a progressive world. We are now beginning to understand that such a belief creates only fear, hatred, and destruction. Precisely the opposite of what is desired. A person or society will behave in accordance to their self-interests as they perceive them and their own belief about reality or their traditions regardless of the external pressure that one puts upon them. And personal and world affairs will continue to use carrot-and-stick diplomacy—always projecting our version of truth upon others.

We must learn it is not possible to make a person work against their deepest self-interests or violate their self-image.

But the important lesson is that the only thing we can really change is ourselves.

Our view of what we are. Our view of

the world around us. To recognize that what we see, what we think, and what we do, corresponded precisely with what we each believe that we are.

The view from space is important to all. Because, for the first time in human history, man has left the bonds of earth and ventured deep into the void of space, leaving behind the limiting confines of our planet. This is not an individual triumph, but a turning point in evolutionary history. We have truly embarked upon a new era for mankind. If we are to become the explorers of space, reaching out from our tiny little planet to explore the immensity of our universe, then we must begin to think of ourselves as being capable of that.

We must abandon the view of ourselves as provincial limited victims of life, accidents of evolution, and start to view ourselves as limitless creatures of God, capable of exploring the vast reaches of space. And capable of knowing what the universe is all about. Only then can we be prepared psychologically to live in this vast, confusing, and complex world we have created for ourselves.

It is very likely that the fact of man's going into space and becoming space creatures, as opposed to worldly earthbound creatures, may have more impact over the next one hundred years than we can possibly see.

But the choice is ours as individuals. We can continue to think narrowly, selfishly, and seeing only that limited view of ourselves. Or we can set about changing our belief, and thus change what we see. Begin to see ourselves in a more expansive, magnificent role. But the choice is ours individually and no one can do it for us. It is ours each and every one.

*For only as we change our belief about
ourselves, and our belief about our reality,
will we start to see what we can become.*

I am reminded of an ancient verse that
serves me well when I lose a perspective
of our higher nature, for it describes the
reality I want to see. It was originally
written in Sanskrit and goes:

> *God sleeps in the minerals*
> *Awakens in the plants*
> *Walks in the animals*
> *And thinks in man.*

LOOKING BACK

In the early 1950s as I was just graduating from college and the Korean War was raging. I was about to be drafted to go to Korea but I chose to enlist in the Navy and to become a pilot. When I finished my college in 1951, I went into the Navy and became a Navy pilot aboard carriers, and then a test pilot. It was in October 1957 when the Soviet Union launched the first artificial satellite, called Sputnik, and I realized at that time—in the Pacific, aboard a carrier—that likely humans would be right behind robot spacecraft. So I set my cap and my goal to go into space if that were to happen. And in that very year, the early astronauts, Alan Shepard, my partner aboard Apollo 14, and his six companions were chosen to be the first astronauts in 1958.

In 1966 I was selected as a part of the Apollo program to go to the moon. I was fortunate to be initially chosen from our group of astronauts to fly aboard Apollo 13. I had been backup on Apollo 10 before that. As circumstances would have it, my partner Alan Shepard came on board Apollo 13 to replace Gordon Cooper. Gordon and I were team mates on Apollo 10 as the backup crew. If you remember, Alan Shepard was the first American in space who made the first suborbital flight in 1963.

But headquarters wanted us to take a little more training time because Alan, unfortunately, had had an inner ear problem and had been grounded for a number of years. He got that corrected and was ready to fly, but they decided to give his crew a little more training time.

So the original Apollo 14 crew, Jim Lovell, Fred Haise, and Ken Mattingly, all friends of mine, were asked to take Apollo 13. We were asked to take Apollo 14. We weren't very pleased with that at the moment, but they got the bad bird that blew up in space, and we got the good bird that got to go on to the moon.

But things did work out in our favor. And I think it probably worked out good for the Apollo 13 crew too, because Ken Mattingly, who was the command module pilot for Apollo 13, got bumped and was replaced by his backup, Jack Swigert, because Ken was exposed to the measles by one of the other crewman's children. And that meant the medics were afraid he would come down with the measles in space and they didn't want to take that chance. Of course, Ken did not come down with the measles, so he was one unhappy guy.

So it turned out—and there's a message in all this—when the hydrogen tank blew on Apollo 13, we had to start immediately toward rescue operations and return these guys to earth. They were two days out on a mission to the moon and still had to go around the moon and come back. Ken Mattingly and I went immediately to the command module and lunar module simulator He was in the command module simulator and I was in the lunar module simulator, trying to solve the problem of how you turn the lunar landing vehicle into a life boat to bring the crew back from the moon. It had never been done before. The equipment in the command and service module, the prime mother ship, was simply not usable. All they could do is come back through the atmosphere, provided Ken could find a way to get them back on minimal amount of battery power, because they were virtually below limits on battery power.

Moral of the story: Ken and I were the two most experienced astronauts in our respective vehicles at that time. And we had to be on the ground to solve their problems for them so that they could get back. If it had been us, I'm sure they would have done the same for us; but a lot hung on our shoulders to get the crew back from space under these very awful conditions. It worked, but I am quoted as saying, "After all was said and done, I believe it was the prayers of hundreds of thousands—no, millions—of people on earth that helped bring that crew back."

We have subsequently learned that thoughts are powerful things that create physical results in the world.

Even though until now we in science did not know that was the case, but now we know it's true. The thoughts, and prayers of millions of people did help get the Apollo 13 crew home.

But then I did fly Apollo 14 with Alan Shepard and Stuart Roosa. Our flight launched in January of 1971. We were sent to the area that Apollo 13 was going to go, called the Frau Mauro highlands.

Our mission was to duplicate that, to land precisely in the area called Frau Mauro, and then do a geology excursion two kilometers away to a crater called Cone Crater, to bring back samples from that, and to set up a science station that had telemetry to send back data to earth.

And I would say, what could an explorer want more than to stand on the pristine surface of another planet where no human has been before? The surface of the moon is a barren, desert-like, magnificently beautiful landscape. It's hard to imagine that a surface with no air, pock-marked with craters and rubble and powder-like dust from being pummeled and pummeled with lava rock into very fine particles over billions and billions of years, is beautiful, but it is. It's magnificent.

But the most powerful thing that happened was on the way home.

My job was being lunar module pilot so I was responsible for the lunar vehicle that landed on the moon and to be the expert on all the lunar surface activities. So when we started home and came off the lunar surface and rejoined the command module with Stuart Roosa in lunar orbit, my job was largely complete. I then functioned as a system engineer, watching my side of the cockpit and the gauges of a well-functioning spacecraft, and it wasn't very challenging at that point. It was very routine as we were coming home after six days in space. My partners had a little more work to do, they were doing experiments, and as a result I had more time to look out the window.

What happened doing that was this panorama of the earth, the moon, the sun, the galaxies, the galactic clusters, the millions and billions of stars was overwhelmingly beautiful. And let me point out to you that in space the heavens are ten times as bright on an entire order of magnitude brighter, and ten times as more stars are visible as ever could be on the surface of the earth, even from the highest mountain on a clear night. It's remarkable. It's only through good telescope photographs of the distant heavens in recent years have we been able to get a decent picture and understanding of the magnificence of the universe we live in, and how full of energy and stars and galactic clusters. It's overwhelming. A totally different picture than we had decades earlier.

What happened was suddenly the recognition that although I could see all these separate things—the galaxies, the planets, the stars, the galactic clusters—in their beauty and in their magnificent profusions—I suddenly experienced them as a commonality, a unity, and connected in some mysterious way.

And I realized that the story of ourselves, as told by our science of that period and even today, is incomplete and perhaps flawed. And the story of ourselves, as told by our cultural cosmologies normally rooted in our religions, is archaic and possibly flawed. And accompanying that new vision was this sense of ecstasy, a peak experience, a wondrous experience. Some of my colleagues who have had this experience have described it as looking on the face of God. As a scientist and philosopher, I tend to ask the deeper questions: "What kind of mind is this that causes this sort of ecstatic view, vision, and understanding?"

This happened for three days coming home. Every time I looked out the window for a few minutes and had the time to contemplate it, this overwhelming sense of bliss was all consuming. I didn't know what it meant. But I did realize that the difference in our scientific cosmology and the cosmology coming from our culture, our traditions, was basically the nature of consciousness, because we don't know what that is or how that came to be because our religions have a certain take on it and our science has a different take on it. And I came back puzzled, overjoyed at the experience, but puzzled as to what it meant. When I got back, I couldn't let go of the question.

The ancients of all cultures have described that experience in one way or another. Throughout all time they have said there's some mysterious connection unifying everything in the universe that is all part and parcel of something that is all one. And we in our science, up until recently have said, no, that's not correct. We only know that things are separate and discrete. But at some deep, subtle level, so the ancient mystics tell us, there is a unity.

When I began doing research in these areas, I realized that every culture in the world had somewhere in their mythology, their history, their folklore, had these experiences where you see things separately, but you feel an upwelling of

joy and bliss, a sense of unity, a sense of
everything as one. And even though that
experience is the same the world over,
the description is different in every
culture.

*And we have religious wars because we
give these descriptions different meanings in
these cultures and then fight over whose
description is the right one.*

LOOKING FORWARD

It is our hope that as we understand ourselves better, and understand our nature and how we fit into the universe better, that we can come to grips with the fact that we are all one in some way. That we are unified. We are all part of the same cloth. When we start to understand this then the need to war, the need for violence, the need to do vicious things to each other, starts to go away.

We need to try to understand each other better. We need to find ways to resolve the continual differences between the haves and the have-nots growing at a greater pace. We need to find ways to resolve the great issues that face us. I stand before you today having worked on this problem for thirty years. It really is a matter, in its most simple form of understanding, of how to create a sustainable civilization.

Every number associated with human activity and development is increasing on an exponential, or geometric, curve. It is growing geometrically every year. At the beginning of the twentieth century this curve turned sharply up. I'm talking about the number of people on the earth, the number of automobiles, the number of airplanes, the number of VCRs, the number of palm pilots and computers and everything else, is on an exponential growth curve. Just how long can you have exponential growth in a finite space?

It doesn't take a genius to understand that you can't do that for very long. But that's what we're doing. But that's the part of the picture we're talking about when we look at earth from space. We start to look at ourselves in a new way. You don't see the disharmony, the violence, the wars going on.

All of us who have been in space describe it as such a harmonious, beautiful little planet. It is only by being here on earth and reading the daily accounts in the newspapers and on the television, and looking at the violence that we see in our cities and the violence between our neighbors and our countries.

Only then do we ask what we are doing to ourselves.

It is well known in psychology that if you put rats in a corner they will fight. And if you push humans too close together, too, they will fight. Unfortunately, the mantle of responsibility to solve some of these problems will fall on your shoulders in a very few years. My generation has been working on this problem for many years and we haven't been doing it very well.

And the worse we do it, the more responsibility is going to descend upon you.

Our prime motivation is to make life better for our children and our grand-children and our neighbors. The emphasis is on our neighbors because we are not very well interconnected. What we have discovered in quantum physics just in the last 20 years is the secret of why the mystics have all said for thousands of years that we are all connected in some mysterious way.

The key is in quantum physics. In quantum physics there are four attributes that are different than what you are learning in your physics and science courses today. These are called entanglement, coherence, non-locality, and resonance.

When you look around, you see things in their separateness. But in the quantum world we learn that if things are in a process together at a subatomic level, they become entangled. And if they go apart, wherever they go across the universe after that, they are inter-connected. And that's called *entanglement.* And their movement is *coherent.* They are entangled with each other.

We thought for 75 years that this really didn't pertain to us: that was theoretical quantum physics that was at the very bottom level of matter. Well it's not. It pertains to us. And when you are entangled in such a way with your mother, your father, your brother, your sisters, and with the folks around you, when you become very close to them, you become in resonance with them.

That means you are sharing information with them at a very subtle level.

Non-locality is a very vital word, because virtually all of the psychic phenomena that have been studied over the years are non-local. What does that mean? It means that you cannot screen out the affect with electromagnetic shielding like light. You can block light, radio waves, you can block out those radiations. What you can't block out is gravitation. It turns out that the subtle telepathy signals cannot be shielded either. They are non-local. That's one of the reasons that conventional science has rejected them— because we have no mechanism to understand it.

It happens to be explainable at the quantum level. This entanglement with non-local, correlated communication is precisely the property of a quantum field and quantum interactions. And that is exactly what humans do.

You will hear people talk about intuition as our sixth sense. No, it is our first sense.

It is rooted in quantum correlation, which was a part of the way our universe was put together long before our planetary environments evolved. And this quantum intuitive sense is the base line. That's where it all starts. And we're just now starting to discover this. You will do well to keep my words in mind because we are opening up an entire field of discovery called quantum biology.

One of the things we are learning is that your belief system biases an experiment.

If you believe certain results will take place, and a colleague in Europe doesn't think the results are valid, the same protocol with both will show that the one who thinks they will get positive results will get positive results. The one thinks they won't get positive results, won't get positive results. And these results were replicated several times to show how our belief about things shapes the outcome of the things we do. That is because our intentionality has an effect.

Part of what these types of practical experiments are showing is that, to a certain extent, we create reality by the way we think about it. And certainly, it is obvious that we create our own reality by the way we react to whatever situation we find ourselves in. So this role of mind in shaping reality is becoming very well established. And we need to learn this, because you get yourself into a lot of trouble just because you think in certain ways. And you get yourself into making choices that are not appropriate choices.

Civilization is at a crossroad. We seem to be doing things to our detriment. We realize that species are being made extinct, the population is growing, the garbage is piling up—all of these ills of civilization seem to be increasing. But since we created most of them, we can undo them and we can solve those problems.

It places the responsibility on each and every one of us to live exactly the type of life and create situations exactly like we would like to see them in this relationship of being harmonious on this planet together. The great patriot Patrick Henry pointed out during the Civil War that we will hang separately or we will all hang together. And that is true right now in our civilizations. We are either all going to work on this together, or we're going down the tubes together.

We can't quarrel with anyone's religion—that is your belief system. All we can do is discover better each day how we fit into this world that we live in. And to point out that we're all interconnected. At the bottom of virtually all religions are these same messages. If you go back in history and study the inner core of virtually all religions, they talk about brotherhood, harmony with nature, love for one another. That is a central message that has come down through the ages in perennial philosophy and in our religions.

What we have tended to do is become radical and forget the core and get all tied up in our ego, and do unpleasant things to each other. That is what we need to correct.

But it depends upon each one of us,

regardless of our faith, to look at the deeper core that says I am a human being, we are all human beings, and we are related to each other on this earth because we are all of the same cloth. And so are the animal species and other life on this planet that we share the planet with. It's up to us to recognize this, to live in harmony with it, and to promote the wellbeing of all life forms.

One of the things that happens with coherent behavior, is that as we learn to develop our own mental capabilities— and meditation is a time-honored tradition—get inside of yourself, quiet the mind, and then start to look beyond that. As you learn to quiet the mind and develop your intuition—those deeper resources and subtle energies in a more profound way—the *resonance* with every-one else starts to take place. And the more that you develop within yourself, the more you will be able to find a harmonious loving relationship with everybody else on earth.

IN CLOSING

Until the day presidents and prime ministers around the globe propose a mandate stating that humankind will make that next giant leap, we will dream and continue to make modest forays into the near heavens. A more ambitious day will inevitably come.

Perhaps it will be our children or grandchildren, or even their children, but one day a craft from this shimmering blue dot will lower into a pale red Martian horizon. Then, gradually, imperceptibly, but inevitably, the shimmering blue dot will slowly recede in the view of the spacecraft that will carry our children's children throughout the ghostly white of the Milky Way.

Still others will follow, and with them the ancient stories of their predecessors. Then they will leave the galaxy in order to make themselves in the image of God.

Edgar Mitchell
The Way of the Explorer

Apollo 14 Astronaut
Navy Captain Dr. Edgar D. Mitchell
(1930 – 2016)

ABOUT EDGAR MITCHELL

Apollo 14 astronaut Edgar Mitchell is one of only twelve men who rode a Saturn rocket all the way to the moon. On February 5, 1971, Navy Captain Dr. Edgar Mitchell became the sixth man to walk on its surface.

On March 1, 1971, he was awarded the Presidential Medal of Freedom by President Richard M. Nixon and was subsequently instrumental in founding the Association of Space Explorers, an organization of astronauts from around the world who have flown in space, formed "to encourage international co-operation in the exploration of science and space and to foster greater environmental awareness."

In October 1997, he was inducted into the Astronaut Hall of Fame. In honor of his contribution to the study of universal awareness and global sustainability, in 2005 Mitchell was nominated for the Nobel Peace Prize. In 2011 he received the da Vinci Award for societal advancement through research and understanding of human consciousness and psyche.

Scientist, test pilot, naval officer, astronaut, entrepreneur, author, and lecturer, Dr. Mitchell's career personifies human-kind's eternal thrust to widen its horizons through the exploration of inner and outer space.

Mitchell passed away February 4, 2016. The missing man formation flown by NASA and the U.S. Navy over his memorial service in West Palm Beach,

Florida, was a moving tribute to a man who gave so much and asked so little.

The missing man formation, known as the "missing angel," is an aerial tribute to military officials, astronauts, veterans, and politicians at a funeral or memorial event. At the precise point of flyover, the center pilot veers skyward in a dramatic 180-degree vertical rise into the heavens signifying the lost comrade. Navy Captain Dr. Edgar Mitchell received this commemoration at the conclusion of his memorial service after his death with hundreds of his family, guests, and NASA colleagues on February 24, 2016, over a verdant park in West Palm Beach, FL.

Carol Mersch, author, journalist, compiler,
and long-time compadre of Apollo 14
astronaut Edgar Mitchell

ABOUT CAROL MERSCH

Carol Mersch, a long-time friend and confidant of Apollo 14 astronaut Edgar Mitchell, is an Oklahoma author and journalist specializing in narrative non-fiction. She has published eight books and numerous articles which she authored and co-compiled with others in areas of space exploration, law enforcement, and spirituality.

Her close friendship with Apollo 14 astronaut Edgar Mitchell led her to develop *The Apostles of Apollo: The Journey of the Bibles to the Moon* (Pen-L Publishing, 2010), for which she was accepted into the Mayborn Literary Guild, and

Reflections of the Moon (Pen-L Publishing, 2013), a book of quotations gleaned from her years of companionship with Mitchell. In 2013, her literary document Religion, Space Exploration and Secular Society was accepted by Taylor & Frances, a national consortium in the UK offering document subscrip-tion services used by museums, libraries, and universities, including the Smithsonian Air & Space Museum.

Prior to this, Mersch was instrumental in publishing several books, including *The Seamless Bible* (Destiny Image, 2004), a chronological presentation of the King James Bible and *The Seamless Gospels* (Destiny Inage, 2005), Coming Home: For Those who Serve and *Those who Wait* (Elm Hill Books, 2004), a devotional/journal for US troops, *Year of Promise* (iUniverse Publishing,

2011), a 365-day devotional/ journal, and *The Heart of a Cop: Stories of Personal Faith from the Line of Duty* (Clovercroft Publishing, 2016).

Her latest book, *Undaunted: The Unflinching Faith, Audacity and Ultimate Betrayal of an American Legend* (Pen-L Publishing), chronicling the life of ordained Presbyterian pastor and NASA Chaplain Reverend John Stout, was released in September 2019.

In 2016, she authored an online long-form article "Trial by Fire" published in The Big Round Table, a platform supported by staff of the Columbia School of Journalism.

Before launching her writing career, she served at the executive level of several Fortune 1000 enterprises and at the helm of three privately-held companies where she received local and national recognition for her contributions to community and civic endeavors.

Mersch has authored numerous articles for national trade and online publications on Information Technology and developed an IT strategy manual utilized by several leading corporations and local governments. She is a high-energy individual who brings integrity and success to any endeavor she undertakes. In 1999 her firm, Mersch-Bacher Associates, was awarded the Blue Star Award for entrepreneurship, and the success of Mersch and her company was featured on a nationally-televised PBS special. In August 2000 The New York Times cited her work in community and civic endeavors.

In 2004, she left the corporate world to form ProvidenceWorks LLC, a business enterprise for developing articles and books "that make a difference."

During this time, she authored, compiled, and co-compiled numerous non-fiction works.

From 2011–2018, Mersch was featured on Houston Fox26, Tulsa ABC NewsOn6, BBC World Radio, Dallas CBS Radio KRLD, MSNBC, CNN Faith, and two magazines in Europe, *Spaceflight Magazine* and *Sorted*—a Christian men's magazine—for her research into the first Lunar Bible covered in her book *The Apostles of Apollo.* The historic Bibles carried to the moon and their heirship have been featured by the Associated Press, the *Houston Chronicle*, the *Baytown Sun*, MSNBC, Fox News, CNN Belief, and *Al Jazeera* "America Tonight" (Sept. 2015).

For more information see
WWW.CAROLMERSCH.COM

Don't miss these fine books

from Carol Mersch

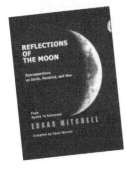

REFLECTIONS OF
THE MOON

"I suspect people will come to honor Mitchell far more in the future when much of what he says proves to be correct. At that time, this book will become even more valuable."

— Author and futurist Stan Schatt

THE APOSTLES OF APOLLO

*The Journey of the Bible to
the Moon and
the Untold Stories of American
Astronauts*

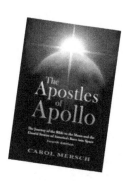

"No one has before written of the Apollo
moon landings in quite the way we see here.
Centering around the story of a project to
put a Bible on the moon, *The Apostles of
Apollo* shows that the greatest feat of
engineering and exploration had its spiritual
side. By going to the moon, men who
believe in God came to better appreciate
the universe that He caused to come
into being."

– Mark R. Whittington

**READ A FREE CHAPTER AT
WWW.PEN-L.COM/
APOSTLESOFAPOLLO.HTML**

UNDAUNTED

The Unflinching Faith, Audacity,
and Ultimate Betrayal of
an American Legend
The Reverend John Stout

He was ordained. He was legendary. The trail of accomplishments he left behind would make grist for an epic movie. Take a former Texas Aggie football player and WW2 officer who was a ballistic missile experimenter who became a Presbyterian missionary and college professor, put him in the wilds of Brazil, liberally add earth satellites and horseback treks among uncivilized Indians, then flavor the whole thing with two American presidents and a Bible that landed on the moon onboard an Apollo spacecraft, and you have the makings of a story any fiction writer would love to get his or her hands on. But this story isn't fiction. It's true. And by his side—every step of the way—was the heart and soul of everything he lived for. Her name was Helen. Reverend John Maxwell Stout is a name to remember.

Dear Reader,
If you enjoyed this
book enough to review
it for Goodreads, B&N,
or Amazon.com, I'd
appreciate it!
Thanks, Carol

Find more great reads at
Pen-L.com

Made in the USA
Monee, IL
03 March 2021

61817161R00059